Learning about
the Bible

by Felicity Henderson
Illustrated by Michael Grimsdale

A LION BOOK

Copyright © 1984 Lion Publishing

Published by
Lion Publishing Corporation
10885 Textile Road, Belleville, Michigan 48111, USA
ISBN 0 85648 523 3 (casebound)

First edition 1984
Reprinted 1984

Text by Felicity Henderson
Illustrations by Michael Grimsdale

Printed and bound in Italy by
Imago Publishing Ltd

Have you ever wondered
how the world began?

Who made the earth?

— and the sky?

— and the sea?

Who made plants?
– and fish?
– and animals?

Who made people?

The Bible tells us
that God made them.

7

The Bible tells us a lot about God.
God looks after the world.
He loves us and cares for us.
He tells us how to live.

The Bible tells us that God sent
his Son Jesus into the world
to show us what God is like.

Do you have a Bible?
It might look like this,

or this,

or this.

It is a very special book.
It was written a long time ago.
People all over the world read
the Bible. It tells an exciting story.

The Bible is a big book.

It is made up of sixty-six smaller books.
(The word 'Bible' means books.)

There are two main parts –
the Old Testament
and the New Testament.

The Old Testament was written
before Jesus was born. It tells us
about God and his chosen people.

The New Testament tells us about
Jesus and what he did and said.
And it tells us about the first followers
of Jesus.

In the Old Testament there are lots
of stories. You may know some of them.
You can read about –

Noah and the ark,

Joseph and his brothers,

Moses, the baby in the bulrushes,

David and Goliath,

and lots of other people.
They are all stories about God
and how good he is.

In the New Testament you can
read about Jesus.
And about his friends – Peter, James
and John and many others.
All of the stories tell us about God
and how good he is.

Some of Jesus' friends were fishermen
on Lake Galilee.

The Bible is full of good stories,
but it is not just a storybook.
It is a very special book.

The stories in the Bible are about real
people and real places – like stories
in history books.
They are important because they tell us
about God.

The Bible says that God is like a good father
to us.
He always loves us, even when we are
naughty.
He is always there.
He is always the same.

There are many books and many stories
in the Bible but they are all part
of one story.

When God made the world,
everything was good.
But people spoilt things by
disobeying God.

After that, God made plans to put
things right.
The Bible tells that story.

The Old Testament tells us how
God loved his people and looked after them.
But often they would not listen to him.

He gave them ten special rules to keep.
We call them the Ten Commandments.

But – just like us – God's people
were not very good at keeping his rules.
Some people did not want to obey God.
This is what we call 'sin'.

So God promised to send his own Son,
the Messiah, 'to save his people from
their sins'.
God sent Jesus.

In the New Testament there are four books
about Jesus.
They are called the Gospels.
The writers were four friends of Jesus –
Matthew, Mark, Luke and John.

The picture shows a story from
John's Gospel.

One day a big crowd followed Jesus.
It was late. They were hungry and had
no food. There were no shops.

A young boy gave away
his own dinner and Jesus shared it
with all the people.
Everyone had enough to eat.

The word 'gospel' means good news.
The Bible says,
'God loved the world so much that
he gave his only Son. And whoever believes
in Jesus will not die, but have a new life,
for ever.'

This is good news.
Jesus died so that we could be forgiven
for the wrong things we have done.
And God raised Jesus to life from the dead.

It is good news for everyone.
It is good news today.

The first followers of Jesus who believed
he was God's Son told other people
the good news. They passed it on.

In the Acts of the Apostles we can read
how these first Christians took
the good news to far-off places.